My name is Peter, and I am a fisherman. My name used to be Simon, but Jesus changed my name to Peter.

Put the sticker of Peter pointing to himself on this page.

1

The first time I met Jesus, my brother Andrew and I were out in our fishing boat. We were using big, heavy nets to catch fish. Wiggly, slippery, wet fish!

Put the stickers of the fishing net and two fish on this page.

Jesus called to us. "Come! Follow me," Jesus
said, "and I will show you how to teach people
about God!"

WOW! I was just a fisherman! Now Jesus
wanted to teach us how to tell people about God.
We left our fishing boat and followed Jesus.

Put the stickers of Jesus and a rock on this page.

One day Jesus told me, "Simon, your faith is as strong as a rock. I will call you Peter because *Peter* means 'rock.' You are Peter, and on this rock I will build my church. You will help me teach people about God!"

Put the sticker of the large rock on this page.

4

Swish, swash, splish, splash. Jesus was carrying a bowl full of water. What was he going to do?

The disciples had traveled a long way on roads of dirt and sand. They had dirty, gritty, smelly feet with sand between their toes!

Put the sticker of Peter with dirty feet on this page.

Swish, swash, splish, splash. Jesus put the bowl of water down on the floor and got down on his knees. Jesus began to wash the disciples' dirty, gritty, sandy, smelly feet.

When Jesus tried to wash Peter's feet, Peter said, "No, Jesus! You will not wash my feet!"

6

Put the stickers of Jesus and the bowl of clean water and towel on this page.

Jesus said to Peter, "Yes, Peter, I will wash your feet."
"But why, Jesus, are you washing my feet?" Peter asked.
"Because I love you," answered Jesus.

Put the stickers of the dirty water and towel
and Peter with clean feet on this page.

7

"Cock-a-doodle-doodle-do!" The rooster crows every morning. Peter loved Jesus. Peter was always trying to do what Jesus wanted him to do. But Jesus told Peter, "Before the rooster crows in the morning, you will tell three lies. Three times you will say that you do not know me."

Put the sticker of Peter looking sad on this page.

8

Page 1

Page 2

Page 2

Page 3

Page 3

Page 4

Page 5

Page 6

Page 6

Page 7

Page 7

Page 8

Page 9

Page 9

Page 10

Page 16

Page 13

Page 10

Page 11

Page 12

Page 14

Page 13

Page 15

Page 16

Peter loved Jesus, but Peter was afraid because some people were angry with Jesus. Peter thought that they might be angry with him too. So not once, not twice, but three times Peter told the angry people that he did not know Jesus!

Then Peter heard the rooster crow, "Cock-a-doodle-doodle-do!"

Put the stickers of the rooster and the tree on this page.

9

Peter was sad because of what he had done. But later Jesus asked Peter an important question, not once, not twice, but three times! Jesus said, "Peter, do you love me?"

And three times Peter could say to Jesus, "Yes, Jesus, you know that I love you."

Put the stickers of Peter standing and talking and the fishing boat on this page.

I have never been able to walk, thought the man lying near the Temple. *I lie here all day long hoping that someone will help me and give me money. I pray that God will send someone to love me and care about me!*

Put the sticker of a man who cannot walk on this page.

11

Just then God sent someone to help. Peter saw the man lying on the ground. The man looked hungry and tired. "Please," the man said to Peter, "give me money for food."

Peter said, "I have no silver or gold, but what I have I give you." The man looked at Peter, and Peter said, "In Jesus' name, stand up and walk."

Put the sticker of Peter reaching out on this page.

Peter reached out and helped the man get up and walk! The man was so excited that he jumped around and danced for joy!

"Praise God! Praise God!" he said.

Put the stickers of a man leaping and dancing and a girl on this page.

13

Peter and Cornelius were different. They ate different foods and went to different churches, but they both loved God. And God loved both of them!

Put the sticker of Peter standing on this page.

14

God told Peter to go to Cornelius's house to teach the people there about Jesus, even people who were different from Peter.

Put the sticker of Cornelius the soldier on this page.

15

Peter taught Cornelius more about God and about Jesus.

Cornelius taught Peter that even people who are different love God.

16

Put the stickers of Peter and Cornelius and a boy on this page.